ASIAN
STYLE

•

EDITORIAL DIRECTION
Suzanne Tise-Isoré and Nathalie Bailleux

ART DIRECTION
Valérie Gautier - Studio Flammarion

TRANSLATION
Deke Dusinberre

COPY-EDITING
Bernard Wooding

•

DESIGN
Caroline Chambeau - Studio Flammarion

PRODUCTION
Claude Blumental

•

Printed and bound by Garzanti, Italy
© Flammarion Paris 2000
ISBN: 2-0801-3680-I
Numéro d'édition: FA 3680
Dépôt légal: April 2000

•

ASIAN
STYLE

GILLES DE BURE

PHOTOGRAPHY BY FRÉDÉRIC MORELLEC

CAPTIONS AND DESIGN BY ANNIE DESGRIPPES

Flammarion

clarity and simplicity

"BEAUTY IS A NAME FOR SOMETHING THAT DOESN'T EXIST, WHICH I GIVE TO THINGS IN EXCHANGE FOR THE PLEASURE THEY GIVE ME."
FERNANDO PESSOA

It feels like a ground swell, a huge, silent breaker: our shores are being swept by Asia—or, to be more precise, by the Far East.

Fashion designers such as Issey Miyake, Rei Kawabuko (from Comme des Garçons), Yojhi Yamamoto and Irié have already opened Westerners' eyes to pure lines, sober colors, simple materials, spare spaces. Their aesthetic approach burst onto the everyday scene in a combination of sophistication and simplicity, composed in a strange and yet familiar way. To a certain extent, exoticism was being tamed, domesticated.

Japanese designers furthermore demonstrated their ability to invent a formal idiom that is astonishingly contemporary yet steeped in tradition, as seen in Sori Yanagi's ideographic stools, Isamu Noguchi's paper lanterns and Shiro Kuramata's curving storage units.

Then came the movies. From Taiwan, Japan, Hong Kong and Shanghai there emerged an extraordinarily complex world (or rather, worlds). Martial arts and tea ceremonies, stateliness and violence, refinement and commonness, universality and specificity suddenly came together in a riot of emblems, objects and spaces—all of them remarkable. Soon the Japanese filmmaker Takeshi Kitano was being feted from one festival to another, while the sublimely beautiful Chinese actress Gong Li was seen on the cover of every magazine in the West.

Beijing, Taipei, Macao, Osaka, Vientiane, Bangkok and Kuala Lumpur henceforth spark the imaginations of Western travelers whose dream destinations had formerly been Venice or New York, Seville or Nairobi, Prague or Machupicchu. Meanwhile, young artists from China, Korea and Japan have been setting the pace at museums of contemporary art and avant-garde art galleries.

The Far East should indeed be considered a paragon of modernity, a hotbed of contemporary experimentation, but this modernity has deep roots and the constant innovation is fed by an age-old classicism.

The pages of this book present an extraordinary view of the world, based on clarity and simplicity, emotion and reason, sensitivity and lofty vision. They will illustrate everyday household objects and aspects of a lifestyle carried to an extreme level of refinement, becoming an art of living in which material and color, shape and pattern are interwoven with a genius for sketchiness, light touches, suggestiveness. Here, effects are so delicate and so universal that they enable every object to inhabit any interior space with harmony and balance, displaying an unmatched economy of means.

Leonardo da Vinci reportedly assured King Francis I of France, "Sire, I will make you cannons as beautiful as they are good." The functional clarity so perfectly expressed by the Renaissance genius applies wonderfully to this series of objects originally from China and Indonesia, Korea and Thailand, Japan and Laos, and even Vietnam. It is accompanied by a kind of spiritual clarity that can be read between the lines of

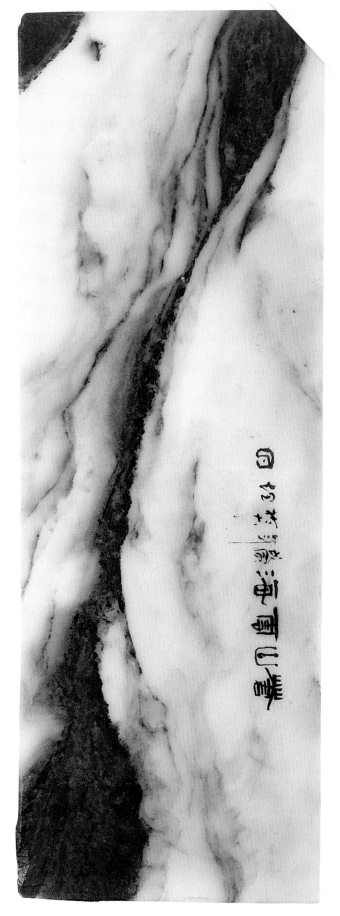

every decision, every gesture. As Goethe put it, "Objects slowly raised me to their level." It is perhaps this unique approach that represents the most accomplished expression of Asian creative genius; a concern for spirituality and simplicity, once again, gives Far Eastern creations universal validity and authenticity.

Interior decorator Andrée Putman, known for her refined, simple taste and her keenness for clarity and significance, recounts a story about André Breton: "Every time the woman who

inspired *Nadja* visited Breton, she left behind a kid glove. This ritual oversight gave Breton the idea of making a cast of it, in its casual pose of abandon. This delightful, absurd object 'works' thanks to its history. Although the stiff cast projects signs of life and movement, you really sense that it sprang from a relationship rather than a mindless desire to be beautiful." Both function and meaning, then, should be clear. Which leads straight to timelessness. Universality and timelessness attune these objects to every place and every era. China, Korea and Japan were already highly fashionable at the French court in the eighteenth century, inspiring the commodes, chests and desks of master cabinetmakers as skilled as Martin Carlin and René Dubos.

Strangely, items from the Far East seem to reject decorativeness. Despite all their materials, patterns, colors and shapes, they project a minimalist stance, a desire for transparence, a concern with defining space through voids, emptiness, or light alone.

They also compulsively erase any sign of effort, eliminate all trace of structure. As Henri Matisse confessed, "I worked for years so that people could say, 'That's all there is to Matisse.'" Matisse himself was highly influenced by Japan, by the elegiac grace of its screens and murals, the evanescence and solidity of its colors, the immateriality and presence of its marks. Attaining that degree of simplicity and sophistication required centuries of attentiveness to the outcome of given methods. It required both modesty and pride.

"Less is more," exclaimed architect Mies van der Rohe, who added that "God is in the details." To which Lao-tse, the Chinese scholar and founder of Taoism, might have replied: "Time has no respect for that which is accomplished without it."

Materials, patterns, colors, shapes—whatever the means of expression, Asian artists and designers always communicate a profound respect for time, duration and permanence.

materials

THE RULE HERE IS: AUTHENTICITY OF MATERIALS ABOVE ALL ELSE. THIS RULE UNSETTLES AND TRANSFORMS OUR WAY OF SEEING THINGS, ASSIGNING EACH MATERIAL A UNIQUE ROLE THAT RESPECTS ITS ORIGINAL NATURE AND IDENTITY. NOTHING ESCAPES THIS CONSISTENT RESPECT, FROM HATS AND BIRCH-BARK ORNAMENTS TO DYED CARP-SKIN CLOAKS (MADE BY SIBERIAN NOMADS), FROM REFINED KOREAN CELADONS TO THE SUBTLEST LACQUERED ITEMS FROM CHINA. CERAMICS COME IN COUNTLESS FORMS, INCLUDING ROUND TILES AND PAVING BRICKS WITH FLORAL DESIGNS, SOME WORKED WITH SUCH FINESSE THAT THEY RESEMBLE LACE. THERE IS LITTLE FURNITURE, REPLACED BY AN INFINITE RANGE OF MATS AND TATAMIS MADE FROM A VARIETY OF MATERIALS, PRIMARILY RICE STRAW.

AND THEN THERE IS A LOVE OF NATURE SO PERFECTLY EXPRESSED—ESPECIALLY IN JAPAN—THROUGH THE ARTS OF GARDENING AND FLOWER ARRANGEMENT. NATURE RECURS IN THE DECORATION OF OBJECTS AND EVEN, PARADOXICALLY, IN THE ABSENCE OF ORNAMENTATION. SOME POTTERY, DEVOID OF DECORATION, IS DELIBERATELY ROUGH—EVEN COARSE—THE BETTER TO EVOKE THE NATURAL FEEL OF ROCK, STONE OR PEBBLE.

WOOD, HEMP, STONE, LEATHER, METAL, EARTH, BAMBOO, RATTAN, STRAW, SILK, PALM LEAVES: NONE ARE CRAFTED, PRODUCED OR REPRODUCED WITHOUT THIS CONSTANT RESPECT FOR THE ESSENCE AND POTENTIAL OF EACH MATERIAL.

There is something deeply fascinating in the way Asia coaxes materials into a kind of immateriality or immanence. They seem pure, graceful, light, impalpable and yet retain such sensuality, such presence, such solidity! Everything here sustains the idea of paradox, sometimes even ambivalence. Matter and materials shimmer. They never seem frozen and, whatever shape they are given, they generate a sense of potential transformation, of ongoing gestation.

A refined touch of transparent, pleated silk lends new subtlety to resolutely contemporary vases (right) even as it echoes delicate lotus flowers (below), the sacred "emblem of Buddhism."

These sensations and vibrations create a strange mystery, lending life to such objects—a life that is simultaneously discreet yet intense, and so authentic that it enables them to reside absolutely everywhere. Wherever they are placed, all of them are able to take shape, to retain all their integrity even as they instantly adapt to their surroundings.

And yet Asia is so vast. Materials and manners differ and change from one land to another.

a multitude

But an elegiac kind of gracefulness always survives, an impalpability endures.

Whatever the material used—paper, wickerwork, clay, stone, bamboo, ceramics, glass, silk, metal or wood—this illusion persists. Take jade, whose realm is China: jade is gentle yet cold to the touch, of remarkable purity and musical resonance, and conveys an impression of such fragility that it instantly sparks emotion; and yet jade is so hard it can bend steel. Jade jewelry is generally highly symbolic in content, taking the

In a nod to the symbolism of Japanese rock gardens, the translucence of this vase underscores the purity of the water in which an exotic Japanese fish swims.

Irregular veins characterize this "dream stone" made of marble from the Dali mountains in Yunnan, which have inspired Chinese poets and artists for centuries.

# of symbols

form of birds, dragons and fish. Although less frequently used for interior decoration, jade objects exist in the form of a disk called *bi* or *pi*, a symbol of the sky whose central hole represents the sun; or as a rectangular block, called *zong* or *tsong*, whose round, inner cylinder symbolizes the Earth.

Though considered a useful object by the Chinese, a *bi* or *zong* of whatever color—green, blue or honey yellow—can be wonderfully decorative when set on a mantelpiece, a wall bracket or low table.

hard yet fragile

A fork and spoon of horn contrast handsomely with a precious table mat made of lacquered silver leaf (above).
A small Japanese bowl of solid stoneware (below). This mosaic of multicolored marble creates a strikingly graphic pattern (right).

Asian interiors feature little or no stone. As for gold and silver, they are usually melted and employed to enhance wood or ceramic; or sometimes they are turned into leaves as fine and translucent as paper, then burned as incense. Or again, leaves of gold and silver may simply be placed in a dish or open box, simultaneously conveying unequaled modesty and richness.

This *lokta* paper represents a blend of two cultures:
made from a wild plant, *Daphne cannabina*,
which grows at an altitude of 10,000 feet in Nepal,
it was carefully pleated by a paper-loving designer in France (left).
A mélange of paper strips, called *saa* in Thailand,
can be made in a range of colors (below).

# of paper

a flutter

A designer devised a mystical, marvelous atmosphere by reproducing
a photograph of Tibetan monks on fine silk, which was wrapped around
a vase of mango wood. The silk creates a perfect illusion of paper (left).

Paper becomes substance when a Japanese concept meets French execution. This elegant presentation box contains various types of plant-based papers (including straw, nettle and leaves) with visible fibers. Each sheet is unique. The clasp—made from perforated stones linked by a strip of leather— adds originality to the object.

The respect for authenticity and the specific nature of each material is wonderfully expressed in the manufacture of paper—or rather, papers, so many and so diverse are they. "We need merely see the texture of paper from China or Japan to feel a kind of warmth that soothes the heart," wrote Jun'ichiro Tanizaki (*In Praise of Shadows*). Paper is made from rice, nettles, straw and leaves of all kinds; plant-fiber papers with multiple, vibrant textures range from Nepalese *lokta* and Thai *saa* to paper made from the leaves of mulberry or mango trees. These countless papers have amazingly multifaceted tones, veins and consistencies.

Such papers are for writing, drawing and painting, of course, but also for arranging and displaying. They can be used in so many ways—as bouquets, place mats, cases, covers, liners. They should be mixed, married and contrasted, provoking unexpected combinations with the sole goal of projecting beauty.

Vegetable confronts mineral—for the ritual of an Oriental bath,
a black pebble of soap embossed with calligraphy is presented on a translucent sheet of rice paper.

In China, small squares of gold and silver paper are burned as incense during funeral ceremonies for a friend or relative. Yet they can add a nice decorative touch to Western interiors (right).

Bound in bright yellow-gold,
this book has a very personal feel. It is made from a dozen sheets of *saa*,
a plant-based paper from Thailand (above).
This Japanese brush, made of natural fibers bound into a little bundle,
is used for modern calligraphy (right).

Just like paper, wickerwork testifies to the incomparable inventiveness of Far Eastern artisans. Rattan, straw and willow bend to Asian imagination in magnificent braids, wondrous tracery, staggering combinations. Whether plain or varnished, Laotian, Chinese, Indonesian and Japanese wickerwork is crafted into items such as baskets and hampers, hats and headrests, mats and sieves, boxes and straps

A roll of Chinese vermicelli and a sheet of rice paper create twin types of translucence (left).
A Chinese shoeshine stool made of bamboo (above).
A rice-paddy hat in varnished bamboo and palm fibers (below).

In our Western homes, all these objects may be used for their original purpose or converted into incomparable decorative items. They need merely be arranged, converted and magnified in a straightforward—rather than exotic—way.

The same goes for pottery, whether Chinese, Korean or Japanese. The oldest and most illustrious ceramics already have their place in the universal history of art. This tradition survives from one country to another with varying specificities, originalities and characters.

earthen works

This little ceramic bowl from China conveys purity of material (right).
The porousness of clay enables the tea leaves in this pot to release all their flavor (below).

egg shells

"Eggshell lacquer-ware" is produced from thousands of tiny pieces of duck egg that are fired, resulting in a crazed, shimmering surface with striking effects of fissure and motion, presence and absence, transparence and opacity. Great decorators were intrigued by this technique in the days of Art Deco, and contemporary designers (who tend to favor purer forms) have rediscovered it.

A dish from Vietnam, in the "eggshell lacquer" technique that appears natural yet mysteriously shrouds itself behind a "secret" fabrication method (left).
The use of natural materials in China is evident in this surprising, branch-like double teapot of baked clay (above)
and in a rice-paddy hat made of waterproof palm and coconut (below).

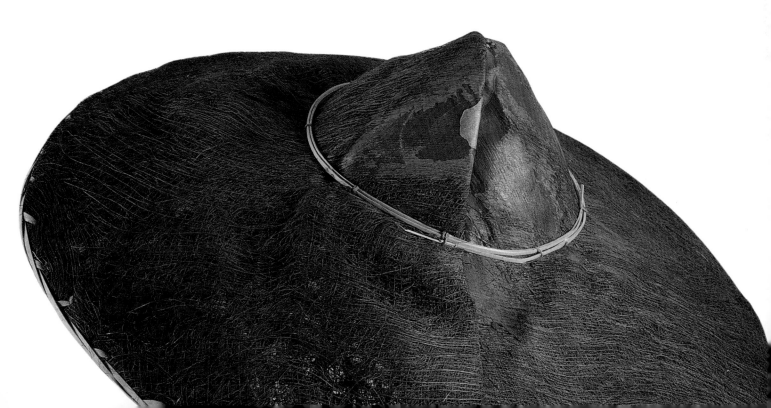

natural weaves

Thanks to natural, vegetable substances, nature enters the home. For an exotic nap, try a Chinese headrest or bolster of braided wicker (above).
When shopping, take a roomy basket woven from bamboo (below). Useful and decorative objects include a cover for a wok (in two-tone straw),
baskets (for fruit, vegetables or laundry), a ladder (for a library), and an immense Chinese sieve originally used for threshing rice (right).

From China comes fine, gray earthenware adorned with red and black circles and spirals, decorated with geometric patterns obtained by pressing the still-soft clay, or graced with deeply etched floral designs. Tiles and bricks may be glazed in extremely subtle hues that yield objects, arrangements, plinths or bases of exquisite beauty.

The brick and tile tradition also exists in Korea, which excels in the art of celadon, a greenish ware that reached its zenith in Korea's incomparably delicate shades of blue, gray and pale olive. Lotus-shaped bowls, eight-lobed wine jars, fruit-shaped vases, incense burners and brush holders may be decorated with inlaid bird or flower motifs. The mere presence of such objects will enliven, enhance and enrich any setting.

Japanese pottery, less ornate than Korean, responds to the local aesthetic ideal, which combines austerity with refinement. Recently, however, more colorful ceramics have appeared in Japan, featuring yellow, deep red and green highlighted with gold and silver. The grand tradition nevertheless favors undecorated stoneware of very sober taste, sometimes glazed in red or black, always magnificently simple, whether vase, sauce jar, pot or plate.

Obviously, given the importance of the tea ceremony in the Empire of the Rising Sun, the most amazing variations on Japanese themes are to be found in tea services. The diversity of tea cups (*chawan*), tea caddies (*chaire*), water jars (*mizusashi*) and incense boxes (*kogo*) is truly infinite.

Used for picking tea, this Laotian basket combines dyed bamboo with willow (left).
A traditional wood steamer, essential for preparing tasty Asian dishes (right).

Japanese cast-iron teapots and kettles present a broad palette of shapes, textures and designs that can be surprisingly decorative, especially when collected in a group. The cast iron is usually black, but is sometimes brown or handsomely tinged with gold, and of course retains the heat. Japan is not very big on the use of metal, and Korea even less so (except when it comes to weapons). Gold and silver are simply used as decorative additions; bronze, meanwhile, is basically used for boxes that contain the sacred scriptures known as *sutras* and, above all, for mirrors (so important in Japan). It was the Chinese who managed to turn bronzework into a major art form: receptacles, vases, urns, cauldrons and goblets are chased, worked and decorated, all attempting to outdo one another in imaginativeness, expressiveness and symbolism.

Wood is worked magnificently in Asia and outstandingly beautiful varieties are used, notably rosewood, sandalwood, teak and cedar. Texture, appearance and scent are the main attributes of a material that the Chinese, Japanese, Laotians, Vietnamese, Khmers and Malays all transform into furniture, obviously, but also, and above all, into receptacles of all shapes and sizes, ranging from travel chests to tiny pill boxes, which represent a decorative find suitable for any setting.

These small, stackable stools in coarse straw will
enliven any modern interior (left).
Sheets of Thai paper in a stack;
Chinese noodles in nests or squares;
a close-up view of coarse straw—all made from
natural plant-based materials (right).

versatile bamboo

Bamboo, a symbol of purity and perseverance in adversity, is greatly honored in Asia.
Even the roots of this surprising plant are usable. Hefty trunks like these (left), topped by hair-like roots,
were the source of this impressive teapot, crafted with rare skill (above).

Dyed wicker baskets carried on the backs of tea-pickers
can also make superb decorative items (right).

taming
nature

A refined, Chinese ceramic plate
shows off a variety of Chinese cabbage (above).
For a contemporary tea ceremony, why not use
a delicate teapot made of glass (right)?

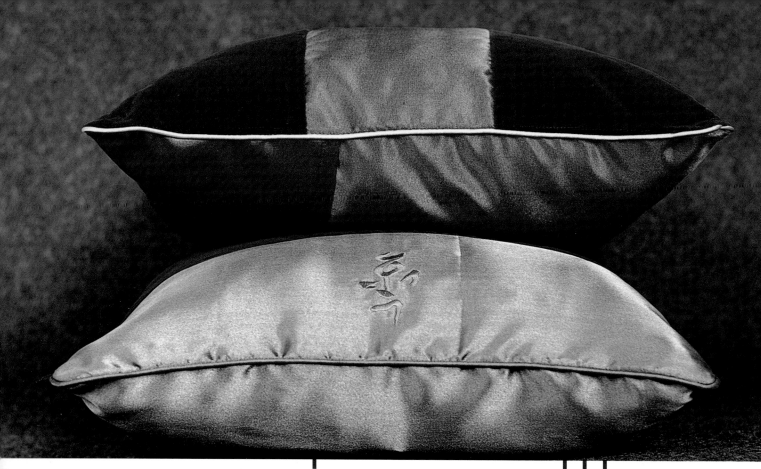

precious silks

The harmonious colors and plush textures of silk pillows and comforters make a nap seem inviting.

Silk must also be mentioned, of course. It is known to date back to the third millennium B.C.E. in China. The Romans, for that matter, called the Chinese *Seres*, meaning people who produce silk. In the early Christian era, China began exporting not only its silks but also artisans able to teach techniques, notably to Korea and Japan. So for five thousand years, the Chinese themselves have been producing unparalleled silks: shimmering colors, refined ornamentation, symbolic patterns, vast dimensions, amazing embroidery, and more.

Silk, stone, earth, metal, wood, paper, fibers, bamboo, bone and ivory all create a symphony of vibrations in lilting shapes, magnificent colors and infinite patterns. Everything is already present in the material—"no matter how it is used," one might be tempted to say. Each object, whatever its shape, color or use, already exudes a presence through the very refinement, the very resonance, the very light of its material. This material is so decorative and expressive in itself that it will immediately find a place anywhere, without sacrificing any of its authenticity.

A precious Chinese dish with unique tones and countless reflections is a delight for the eye as well as the palate (left). A tea ceremony calls for a cocktail of materials—cast-iron for the teapot and saucers, ceramic for the little cups, lacquer for the tray, and silk for the pillows… not forgetting the Chinese nougat (below)!

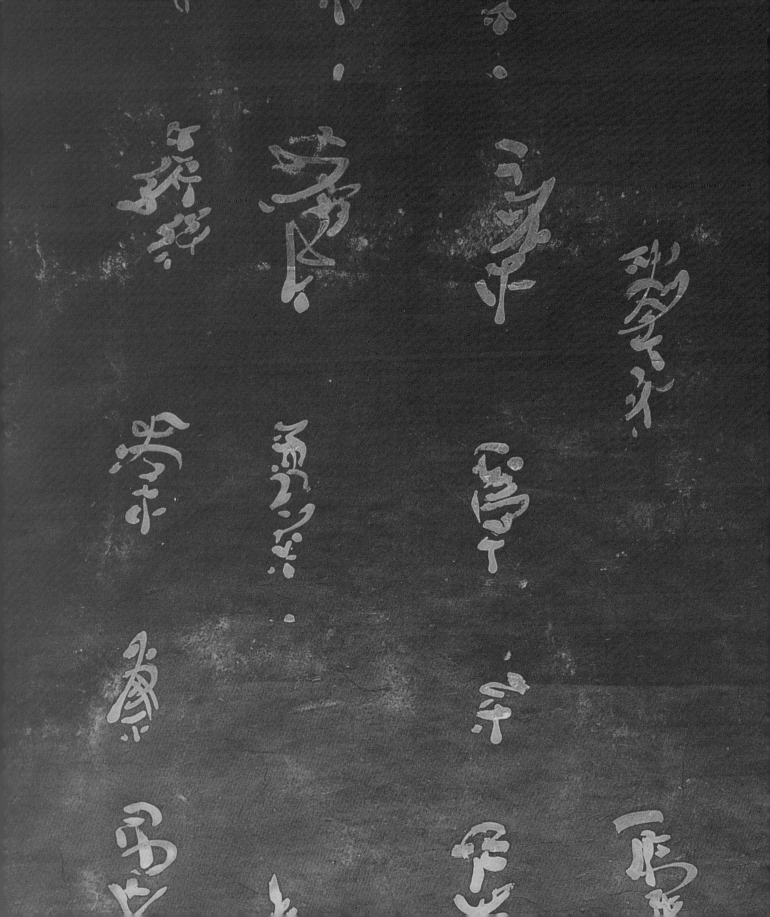

colors

A PASSAGE IN *THE TALE OF GENJI*—A CLASSIC OF JAPANESE LITERATURE WRITTEN IN THE EARLY ELEVENTH CENTURY BY MURASAKI SHIKIBU— DESCRIBES THE APPEARANCE OF A GENJI PRINCE: "WHEN HE WORE A SUMMER *NOSHI* WITH A FINE RED CLOAK, THE EYE NEVER WEARIED OF LOOKING AT HIM, ALTHOUGH HE WAS THIN AND WEAK."

BY THE TENTH CENTURY IN JAPAN, IN FACT, HIGHLY EXTREME REFINEMENT WAS ALREADY DISPLAYED IN GARMENT FABRICS, WHETHER HEMPEN OR SILK. THIS REFINEMENT WOULD BE SEEN IN THE *KOSODE*, THE FORERUNNER OF THE KIMONO, REACHING ITS ZENITH IN COURT DRESS, AS WONDERFULLY EXPRESSED IN *NOSHIS*, A FULL GARMENT WORN BY NOBLEMEN.

THE DEPLOYMENT OF RICH COMBINATIONS OF PURE, BRIGHT COLORS CAN BE FOUND THROUGHOUT THE FAR EAST, NOT ONLY IN CLOTHING BUT ALSO IN HOMES. ONCE AGAIN, IT ENTAILS A SYMBOLISM THAT IS EXTREMELY SUBTLE AND SKILLFULLY CODIFIED.

WHITE IS THE SYMBOL OF PURITY AND LIGHT. BLACK IS THE SYMBOL OF MYSTERY AND ELEGANCE, BRILLIANCE AND INTENSITY. RED, BLUE AND GREEN JOIN IN AN ESOTERIC PLAY OF CORRESPONDENCES WITH WATER AND FIRE, EARTH, WOOD AND METAL. AND FINALLY, YELLOW IS THE IMPERIAL COLOR, USED AS THE BACKGROUND OF MANY FABRICS ON WHICH ARE SET MYRIAD TRACERIES OF RED, BLUE, GREEN, BLACK AND PINK.

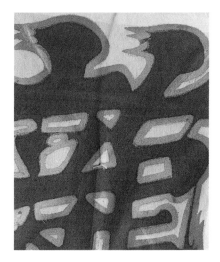

cinnabar red

Red, symbol of fire and creation, plays a dominant role in Asian culture, especially in China (above, a detail from a Chinese kite).
Various shades of red are seen in this clutter of traditional furniture and objects—an aged buffet with side wings,
a nineteenth-century make-up case and tub, baskets for offerings, a lacquered picnic basket,
tea caddies, Chinese headrest, and a tea tray with ceramic teapot and cup (left).

In waves of blue and black, a human tide rolls up the Bund, the vast dockside avenue lining the port of Shanghai. There are thousands of them, all dressed in blue, legs energetically pumping the pedals of big black bicycles. Their blue "Mao suits" first arrived in France via Marseille, sweeping the land during the events of 1968. They formed a vast blue background that the Cultural Revolution splashed with millions of red dots, namely the *Little Red Book* of sayings and thoughts of Chairman Mao.

The deep red lacquer of these stackable plates, salad bowls and boxes requires the delicate application
of several layers of varnish, every one sanded to a perfect finish (previous pages).
Complementary contrasts arise from the round simplicity of these little fur-ringed Chinese slippers
set against the elegance of a Japanese paper parasol (above and right).

As soon as China is mentioned, Western imaginations see red and blue. Red, of course, is the color of blood and therefore of life. And cobalt blue has, in a way, become the trademark of Chinese goods ever since the Mongol invasion of 1276. This cobalt blue was sometimes called "sapphire blue" and was exported around the world, notably in the form of wonderfully beautiful ceramics.

And yet this vast, mysterious, solemn China is in fact composed of a multitude of colors skillfully arranged, perfectly controlled and modulated.

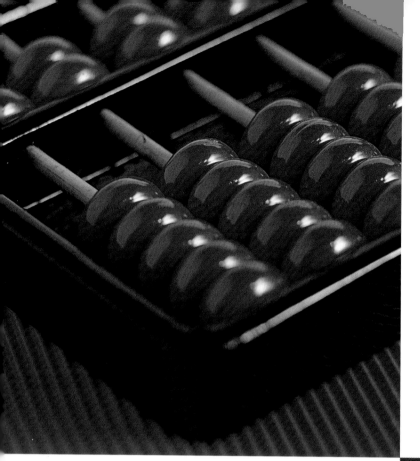

An old Chinese tub in bright red,
perfect for an infant's bath under the watchful eye of a
long-necked bird (right).

Although some Asian merchants still use an abacus, this traditional
item in red lacquer is also a fine decorative object in itself (above).
Also red are these very elegant hairpins designed to offset
the jet-black hair of Japanese women (right).

azurite and indigo

Asian tradition assumes an operatic air—shoes awaiting ballerinas and an openwork fan of sandalwood,
set on a Chinese shoeshine stool.

Color has played a crucial role in the history of the decorative arts in the Middle Kingdom from earliest times down to today. Colors are above all vegetable and mineral in origin: white was made by grinding freshwater shells; blue from indigo or azurite; red from cinnabar and ocher; yellow from gamboge and orpiment; green from malachite, black from charcoal and charred bones. The Chinese first elaborated their palette on the walls of their houses. Thanks to their strong love of color, that palette was subsequently enriched by brown, pink, purple, orange, gold, silver and a wide range of ochers. Very swiftly, Chinese artisans became past masters in the play of analogy (that is to say, monochrome shades) and contrast (complementary colors). They then went further by systematically playing on oppositions between warm and cool tones, light and dark hues. They also brought black and white into the game, which the Chinese consider to be colors in their own right.

Formerly, incense was burned only in stately residences or in honor of the gods.
Nowadays, every home can benefit from these natural, exotic fragrances—but before burning the sticks,
why not allow the decorative bundles to add a note of color to a room?

In China, monochrome ceramics enjoyed great prestige, notably during the Tang and Song dynasties. Chinese monochrome pottery in blue, ivory white, cucumber green, blood red, ocher yellow or violet would be enameled, glazed, oxidized or painted—but never left translucent, as in the West.

imperial yellow

Phosphorescent twists of Thai paper create a flamboyant blend of gold and light (left). The luminosity of "imperial yellow" vases, set directly upon the parquet floor, lends a sunny sparkle to this sober setting (right). Contemporary transparency and reflections: this round, glass teapot, endowed with an ingenious steeping system, seems a long way from traditional Chinese or Japanese teapots, whereas the shimmering, colorful glasses feature a slightly bowed curve that recalls bamboo (following pages).

iridescent
transparence

Instead, Chinese potters obtained lightness and intangibility through the play of color. Chinese monochromes prove to be of great complexity and great refinement. The same piece can range in hue from profoundly dense to subtly pale. Certain tones may be velvety, while others mask decoration in such low relief that it practically has to be intuited.

The challenge was to rival nature and match her complexity and subtlety. Such meticulous yet inspired work yielded striking results

sapphire blue

Under the Ming dynasty (1368-1644), the Chinese developed and perfected their fabulous "blue-and-white china," based on a pure, deep blue of infinite variation. Wonderful, fascinating shades of this one color—ranging from pale gray to purple blue—can be seen in china decorated in various patterns featuring calligraphy, ideograms, birds, fish, flowers and leaves.

that would be dubbed, for example, "the color of the sky after rainfall."

The same concern can be found among the Japanese, who would sometimes seek to produce a "snowflake" effect from simple white porcelain, and who adopted—as did almost all the peoples of Southeast Asia—the famous "blue and white" of the Chinese.

Shimmering colors were used less for the home and household objects than for fabrics and garments. This was notably true of court and state dress, which was embroidered in gold and silver or enhanced with precious gems, but it was also true of flamboyant silks in which all

combinations were not only permitted, but required—an orgy of color that spilled into the cotton and woolen fabrics that the Chinese also knew how to dye, print and stencil. Then there were the carpets, mainly of yellow and blue, which covered the floors. Little by little, China would export its love of color to Korea and, especially, Japan.

Although austere—even strict—Japan indulges in fanciful wall paintings and frescoes in temples and the occasional castle, featuring gods with

gold finery

pale yellow bodies dressed in robes and scarves of deep red, orange, blue and green. But Japanese architecture of wood and paper, with few dividing walls, is little conducive to color. So color first took wing on folding screens, screens with magnificent gold grounds, dotted with pink and white peonies.

Color then spread to fabrics and garments, in an equally bold and more pronounced manner than in China, if less ornate. Kimonos and *noshis* featured an extraordinary display of rich, lively hues. *Obis*, the broad sashes with large knot in the back, provided an opportunity for stunning polychromatic experiments. Yet it was on squares of silk embroidery (*fukusas* or *furoshiki*), which were used to wrap a box containing a message or gift, that the use of color achieved a richness as dazzling as it was harmonious and subtle.

The Far East, then, employs a multitude of colors: imperial yellow, pure light-filled white, mysterious and elegant black, plus—now and forevermore—red and black together. Black glaze of smoke, red glaze of cinnabar, black on the outside, red on the inside: here, in red and black, are the keys to the lacquer empire in which the Chinese and Japanese excel.

A black and gold setting adds luster to fruit-flavored tea leaves (left) and a bench in Chinese elm (right).

Lacquer work reached its zenith during the Han dynasty in China. Meticulous, patient work might entail up to thirty layers of applied lacquer, with several weeks of drying required between each layer. And with each layer, the threat of cracks or crazing could bring everything to naught.

Lacquer was red and black—at least for receptacles and furniture. Red and black would be inlaid with gold, silver and mother-of-pearl, picking up light, reflections, insubstantiality, weightlessness. Lightness, hollowness and void were designed to offset opacity, strength and richness.

black as ink

A traditional Japanese teapot in cast iron (left).
A highly refined lacquer powder case with silver inlay flowers (below).

In short, this unmatched refinement always involves a paradox: everything and its opposite should be equally important.

Monochromatic color is exploited down to its last resources of opacity and transparence; polychromatic color leads to highly subtle associations and to bold clashes.

Asia offers the most wonderful of palettes— imaginative derivatives, blends of stunning virtuosity, endless combinations, confrontations and disjunctions.

white

opalescence

White, symbol of purity and light, evokes a serene, peaceful, quiet world.

patterns

FROM JAPANESE YAKUZAS TO MAORI RUGBY PLAYERS VIA MALAY PIRATES AND MONGOL HORSEMEN, TATTOOS HAVE GIVEN BIRTH TO AN IMAGERY THAT IS NOW A WORLDWIDE FASHION THANKS TO MOVIES AND TV. BUT THE FASHION FOR TATTOOS HAS RESTRICTED ITSELF TO THE IMAGE ALONE, TO THE MARK, TO THE VAGUE AND UNCERTAIN SIGN OF RECOGNITION. GONE ARE THE SIGNS OF BELONGING, THE SYMBOLIC SIGNIFICANCE, THE COSMIC DIMENSION.

IN ASIA, WHERE THE JAPANESE BROUGHT THE ART TO ITS HEIGHT, THE VISUAL VOCABULARY OF TATTOOING WAS ADAPTED TO THE HUMAN BODY. ABSTRACT AND NATURALISTIC DESIGNS WERE ORCHESTRATED MASTERFULLY THROUGH SYMMETRY, REPETITION, INVERSION, ALTERNATION, ASYMMETRY AND JUXTAPOSITION.

THIS VOCABULARY IS SPECIFIC UNTO ITSELF, YET REFLECTS VARIOUS INFLUENCES; IT OWES A GREAT DEAL TO THE LINEAR SIMPLICITY TYPICAL OF NOMADIC INVADERS FROM THE STEPPES OF CENTRAL ASIA; TO INDIA, WHICH CONTRIBUTED LOTUS BUDS AND BUTTERFLIES ALONG WITH BUDDHISM; AND TO SASSANID ARTISTS WHO, FORCED OUT OF PERSIA BY ISLAM, BROUGHT TO CHINA THEIR FOLIATE SCROLLS, PALMETTES, SYMMETRICAL GARDEN FLOWERS AND ARTISTIC FRIEZES.

THROUGHOUT THE FAR EAST, THIS SERIES OF PATTERNS CAN BE FOUND IN BOTH ARCHITECTURE AND INTERIOR DECORATION, ON POTTERY, WOOD, METAL AND TEXTILES. AND ITS SYMBOLISM REMAINS INTACT, WHETHER EXPRESSED WITH EXTREME AUSTERITY OR THE MOST FLAMBOYANT EXTRAVAGANCE.

floral figures

A marriage of the precious and the casual: flowerpots with calligraphy enhance the fragile grace of Christmas roses (above), while a rustic lunch-box is enameled with stylized roses (right).

Multiple influences and inspirations mingle here, with a tendency toward the abstract and the geometric. In fact, it is more a question of synthesis than abstraction, from the geometric patterns on silks embroidered by Siberian Yakuts to Indonesian chevron designs via the diagonal S and Z designs specific to China and Japan. It provides a way—or rather, ways—of fully imparting movement and rhythm.

This round box features a rich floral composition. Mother-of-pearl inlay enlivens the decoration and makes it shimmer (above).
A close-up of a pattern on a silk Japanese *obi* underscores the fine gold and beige weave of chrysanthemums and Oriental plane leaves.

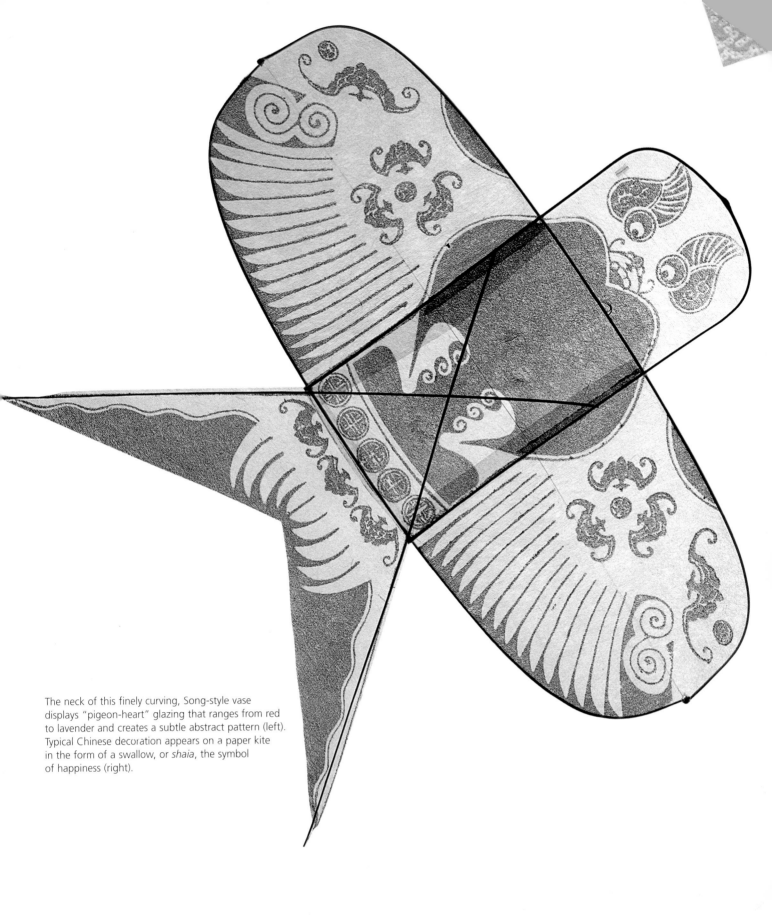

The neck of this finely curving, Song-style vase
displays "pigeon-heart" glazing that ranges from red
to lavender and creates a subtle abstract pattern (left).
Typical Chinese decoration appears on a paper kite
in the form of a swallow, or *shaia*, the symbol
of happiness (right).

The art of patterning here entails true skills of synthesis, often accompanied by an absence of depth in the design, the better to underscore the surface. This approach notably influenced Art Nouveau and Modernism in the early twentieth century.

Powerfully sober compositions, a dazzling wealth of colors and inexhaustibly fertile imagination all contribute to a cosmogony of patterns that can be expressed through such techniques as weaving, printing, stenciling, woodcutting and embroidery.

This extreme synthesis engenders highly specific local variations from one country to another, plus a symphony of symbols both ·cosmological

(heaven, earth, sun, cardinal points, constellations) and natural (flora and fauna).

Thus in Japan, emphasis is placed on asymmetry and the use of undulating rhythms, the better to wed fields of quivering flowers to magnificent, solid backgrounds. In contrast, although Korea also exhibits a marked taste for undulating patterns, they are designed to create a simple, sustained rhythm.

So there are thousands of codes, all with strange and fascinating meanings. And then there is calligraphy—everywhere. It is considered to be the first among arts in the East, which explains why ideograms so often crop up as decorative motifs.

What should be noted among this roster of patterns? First of all, point and line: points, when repeated, orchestrated and juxtaposed, compose endless fields; lines are often used as bands to separate two more complex or naturalistic patterns.

Then come zigzags, which symbolize water; followed by chevrons, tracery and curves; the coils commonly seen on Japanese blazons; loops and spirals (which, when given sharp edges, symbolize lightning); and ellipses.

There are also geometric figures such as squares, diamonds, rectangles, triangles, hexagons and

These table napkins, with their pastel tones and pointillist patterns, are as delicate in color as they are in texture (far left). The colors and patterns of the floral wrappings of these Chinese bars of soap indicate the scent (left). Harmony and contrast are evident in this modest Chinese thermos with its charmingly naive decoration (right).

Flowers are set against a pattern of fans in a venerable kimono that features chrysanthemums in the purest Japanese tradition (above).
A close-up view reveals the finesse of this wonderful silk damask weave (right).

octagons. Geometric figures can also have a highly symbolic and naturalistic content.

Thus a triangle represents a mountain, a circle the sky and a spiral the movement of heavenly bodies. A circle divided by an S-curve symbolizes yin and yang, the male and female entities.

These multiple meanings are accompanied above all by inventive combinations and imaginative juxtaposition that generate purely decorative ensembles of astonishing variety.

point and line

This same inventiveness and imaginativeness are found in the combination and juxtaposition of naturalistic motifs featuring, in addition, an economy of means and art of effacement that drive naturalistic realism toward a kind of heraldic stylization.

A lacquered, papier-mâché lunch pail displays harmonious proportions matched by a handle that frames the shape. Each compartment is separated by a ring of wood (left).
A velvet pillow, its satin band embroidered with an ideogram, is perfect for a cushy sofa (right).

The most prominent motifs are from the natural world, with lightning and stars, rain and clouds, waves and flames forming an endless ballet of curves, undulations, bends and spins. The vegetable kingdom flaunts its processions of leaves and flowers, featuring gingko and paulownia boughs, plum and apple trees, mulberry and plane leaves, lotus and

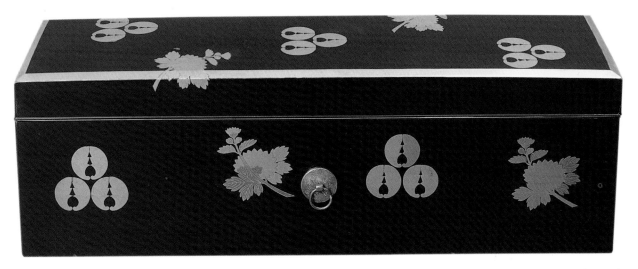

Two small, ancient Chinese lanterns with elaborate mesh are lined with calligraphic paper, creating an intimate chiaroscuro effect (left).
An antique box in black lacquer features harmonious repetition of geometric and plant motifs (above).
Deflected from its original use as wrapping silk, a delicate-hued *furoshiki* with butterfly pattern can become
an elegant scarf; an ideogram decorates a collapsible Japanese lantern (following pages).

chrysanthemum flowers, peonies, orchids and roses. There is also an outstandingly rich animal kingdom, featuring first and foremost real animals, ever-present and usually viewed as friends or protectors (for example, the Buddhists' faithful elephant and China's ubiquitous fish, notably carp).

butterflies of light

In Japan and China, birds were popular motifs (especially cranes and ducks, together with butterflies), and in Burma, Thailand and China, tigers were common. Other motifs include: the cicada, symbolizing resurrection; the diaphanous Japanese dragonfly; the swallow, harbinger of happiness; and the peacock who, wings spread and tail raised like a multicolored bouquet, provides an occasion for stylistic exploits of unmatched refinement and preciousness.

the art of calligraphy

Then there is an imaginary bestiary that welcomes endless variants and distinctions, dominated by dragons and phoenixes depicted so variously, so imaginatively, that it is almost impossible to list them all. Yet a dragon always symbolizes rain, fertility and procreation, while a phoenix represents strength, beauty and happiness.

This Japanese goat-hair brush remains very supple when applied to the inking stone (left). Sturdy flat pencils used by Chinese carpenters must be sharpened with a knife (right). Gifts can be presented in "calligraphic wrapping" thanks to the simple use of newsprint.

To this bestiary must be added China's own *tsao-tié*, a terrifying mask of an animal with horns, bulging round eyes and menacing fangs. Tsao tié, literally meaning "glutton," symbolizes animal strength and, consequently, protection against evil spirits. Although symbolic vocabulary may shift and overlap from Japan to Tonkin, from Korea to Burma and from Cambodia to Indonesia, China still provides its crucible and its apex.

The same is true of calligraphy, which highly civilized peoples have always employed to decorative ends, whether involving Egyptian hieroglyphs, Arabic script, or Chinese and Japanese ideograms. Calligraphy is considered the first among arts by both the Chinese and the Japanese. It embodies the origin and outcome of ideas and gestures, being "ideographic" in the sense of combining idea and gesture in a single sign. In China and Japan, the art of calligraphy has attained a unique level of perfection, especially given its countless variations. Thus, for example, the Chinese word *shou*, meaning "long life," can be written in over one hundred different ways when used as a decorative motif.

Calligraphy is not always used for purely decorative reasons. It is also employed for greetings and messages of happiness and

A Chinese calligraphy scroll is painted on silk, backed with rice paper. The inscription means "goodness and kindness." The artist's signature figures on the lower right side (left).
A perfect curve is displayed by a large vase with red and black calligraphy of varying sizes (right).

和平處事

意時提出明天的希望，在仇恨

傷時贈予喜悅的安慰。在懷疑

恨處散播慈悲的種子，在失意時

恨處施予寬恕的諒解，在

恨處施予寬恕的諒解的諒解，在

在黑暗

在失意時

在懷疑

prosperity. This explains the importance of deciphering the calligraphy on any object you may own: that way, idea and gesture will be reunited once again.

In fact, the symbolism behind Asian decoration often converges with Western symbolism. The same meanings, at least, may be expressed through different signs. In Japan, for example, the patterns on silver hairpins worn by young women indicate their status—unmarried, married, widow, etc.—just as the shape of European signet rings—square, oval, diamond—communicate a rank along with a family's historical and geographical background. In this respect,

Strong graphics grace a packet of Chinese vermicelli (left).
A Japanese brush of horse hair (right).
The inscription on this small square kite means "dragon" in Chinese (below).

Japanese blazons are extremely simple: always inscribed in a circle, they tolerate no encumbrances such as supporting animals, crowns or helmets, and are often placed on the hilts of swords which, for that reason, are also round. Floral motifs abound here, too, such as the sixteen-petaled chrysanthemum (for the imperial family), a paulownia branch or a mauve leaf.

These timeless designs, whether geometric or naturalistic, are always symbolic. Extremely flexible and versatile, they adapt admirably to every surface, every material, every shape. Such timeless patterns are constantly revitalized through combination, juxtaposition and contrast. In addition, the Asian artist's sense and love of color will add yet another new dimension every time.

Although timeless, these patterns seem amazingly modern, strangely contemporary. In Korea, it is not unusual to find a vase, kite or kimono with decorative patterns that inevitably recall the work of today's abstract and conceptual artists.

These patterns suggest, celebrate and symbolize dramatic or everyday events in a symbolic blossoming that can be interpreted at the stately pace of passing seasons: in the Far East, chrysanthemums greet and represent autumn; the wild apple tree, winter; peonies, spring; and lotus flowers, summer.

Old, perfectly shaped bowls decorated with Chinese ideograms.

heavenly circles

With its bold geometric design, this kite made by a Korean master constitutes a veritable work of art (left).
A swarm of multicolored bubbles gives this ancient kimono a resolutely contemporary feel (above).

like
a cloud of fireflies

A Chinese swallow kite is decorated with naturalistic designs (butterflies and chrysanthemums) often used in China (left).
The innocence of these authentic, translucent Chinese lanterns with their colorful floral decoration is sustained by a sheer, spring-like curtain (right).

This calligraphic design was brushed in hot wax onto Nepalese paper, then spray-painted.
It is the work of a contemporary artist who divides his time between France, Japan and Nepal (left).
The stylized fish decorating this enameled metal dish follows the curve of the plate (above).

shapes

HIGHLY REFINED SHAPES OF INTENSE SIMPLICITY YIELD A VOCABULARY OF LEGIBILITY, OF PRECISE PROCEDURE, OF INSTANT CLARITY; YET, AT THE SAME TIME, THEY EMBODY A COMPLEXITY THAT ENDOWS EACH OBJECT WITH MULTIPLE FUNCTIONS, A VARIETY OF USES FROM THE MOST ORDINARY TO THE MOST SOPHISTICATED. EVERY SHAPE SEEMS TO BE A HYMN TO PURITY, A LESSON IN EXTREME REFINEMENT.

BOXES, CASKETS, WRITING CASES, BOWLS, COMBS, BRUSHES AND HOUSEHOLD ACCESSORIES ARE ALWAYS PRACTICAL YET ENDOWED WITH SUCH GRACE AND ELEGANCE THEY SEEM DESIGNED FOR PURE DELIGHT. THIS IS ESPECIALLY TRUE OF THE LITTLE BOXES MADE FOR FOR PILLS, COSMETICS, SCENT, MIRRORS, ALL OF WHICH TESTIFY TO AN UNMATCHED ARTISTRY AND MASTERY OF WOODWORKING.

FURNITURE—OF WHICH THERE IS LITTLE BECAUSE ASIANS OFTEN SIT AND SLEEP ON THE FLOOR— IS USUALLY LOW AND CONSISTS OF SMALL TABLES, CHESTS AND ASYMMETRICAL SHELVING.

WHETHER REFINED OR PRIMITIVE, FURNISHINGS AND OBJECTS DISPLAY SMOOTH, GRACEFUL CURVES, TO WHICH THEIR CREATORS—ARTISTS, ARTISANS OR DESIGNERS—MANAGE TO IMPART LINEAR DYNAMISM AND A THOROUGHLY REMARKABLE SENSE OF RHYTHM.

In Asia, each object acquires formal beauty from its sense of balance as much as from its decoration. Purity of line, quality of material, and harmony of colors and patterns are all essential. Everything depends on this balance, born of the confrontation between vertical and horizontal lines on the one hand, or diagonal and curving lines on the other. In this respect, it is fascinating to realize that the word "decoration" does not exist in Japanese. Japanese architects will refer, in their native language, to "interior design" to describe a barely distinguishable concept. For them, life is a whole: every shape and form is simultaneously a part, the sum and an abbreviation of that whole.

refined lines

The earliest folding fans appeared in China in the late ninth century, when they hung from belts. They were made from slats of bamboo, tortoiseshell or ivory, across which rice paper or silk was stretched. One side would be painted with motifs such as flowers, birds or bamboo shoots, while the other side would feature calligraphy. Many artists graced fans with their work, sparking the enthusiasm of collectors. The one shown here is Japanese in origin (left). A very contemporary interpretation of Japanese bedside lanterns—the stands are made of raw metal while the austere lanterns are stretched with parchment (right).

Milky opalescence and rainbow reflections enhance the pure lines of these modern goblets (left).
The mysterious glow of these opaline stones is refined by the gold of very thin paper.—their shape recalls
the round pebbles used in Japanese rock gardens (above).

The harmonious proportions of these Song-style bowls have rarely been equalled, and are worthy of their twelfth-century forebears (above). These little white pebbles in fact serve as knife-rests; they are shown here on a frosted glass tray of similar purity (below). Five carefully arranged "stones" of brushed metal yield a zigzagging candle holder (right).

In China, on the other hand, decoration truly exists. Two recent films, Chen Kaige's *Farewell My Concubine* and Hou Hsiao-hsien's *Shanghai Flowers,* give an idea of its range: dense and opulent, simultaneously dark and sparkling in the way black and red—lacquer and lantern—weave a phantasmagoria of shadow and mystery. It might be a kind of distant, exotic version of late-nineteenth-century French rococo ornamentation, or of those extravagant, early-twentieth-century palaces built by Turkish potentates along the Bosphorus. Here, it is the accumulation of shapes and colors (often highly refined) that creates the sense of profusion.

Perfectly harmonious and balanced, often monochrome, the finest Chinese pottery, descended from Song dynasty ceramics produced in the twelfth and thirteenth centuries, represents the height of simplicity. Three-legged cooking vessels, jugs and vases with carved or inscribed decoration, amphoras with dragon-shaped handles, wide-mouthed vases, bowls with covers (sometimes gadrooned), dishes with garlanded edges: most of the time, these are robust ceramics designed to be used.

elegant curves

This "butterfly" stool, devised in 1956 by Japanese designer Sori Yanagi, has become a classic piece of furniture that fits every interior—as its name suggests, the shape is as light as a butterfly.

Nevertheless, each of them is conceived, planned and created in such a way that it attains near perfection, so that it immediately fits into a space. The same is true of the large, powerful vases and square, four-legged bowls so typically Japanese which, once set down—the former on a parquet floor, the latter on a table—instantly seize the space and transfigure it.

In the sphere of everyday objects, the Chinese give freest rein to ornamentation when they work in metal. Although objects perform the same functions when made of metal, their shapes become richer, more complicated and more indiscreet.

This mysterious receptacle, with its refined, Japanese-style lines, is designed to hold containers of ice cream.
It is made of biscuit—porcelain that is fired twice but left in a mat, unglazed state (left).
A set of nesting bowls by a contemporary Japanese glassmaker recalls certain Japanese rock gardens.
Their satiny black color lends great refinement. The stone is made of black-tinted glass (above).

This is amply demonstrated by, say, a dish in gold with a handle in the shape of a rampant lion or tiger, or a many-lobed tray of silver. Further demonstration is provided by bronze pots and vases in animal shapes, where elephants, owls, rams and tigers all jostle for the lion's share.

Alongside these realistic animals, which constitute a rich, remarkably graphic ornamental tradition, there are also fantasy creatures like the *kouei*, a dragon with long tail and crest. Such animals also appear in China in extremely stylized form, in the shape of white porcelain teapots. These are often based on the elephant, whose trunk makes an ideal spout.

Further east, in Japan, cast-iron teapots are the object of incredible formal variations. To a certain extent, metal and porcelain are opposites: porcelain is expected to adopt pure, self-sufficient forms, while metal is thought to provide a field day for stylistic and formal exploits.

This was also true for the jade of yore, insofar as working jade symbolized a way to defy time: jade is so hard and resistant that it sometimes takes the finest carvers years to transform the stone into a jewel, amulet, or little ornament for sword or belt. The difficulty of carving jade explains both the diminutive size and the high cost of such items.

This fine celadon stoneware was produced
in France along Japanese lines (left).
A simple yet refined "elephant" teapot
is made of white porcelain (right).

The pure tradition of strong graphic lines is reflected in white porcelain chopsticks and plate set on a glass tray (left). These small Chinese spoons were inlaid with grains of rice (above).

The bestiary of jade objects—swimming carp, flapping cormorant, standing bird with openwork crest and tail, entwined dragons, symmetrical phoenixes—contains, as always, its symbolic charge, while its complexity and finesse indicate the rank of its owner.

structured frameworks

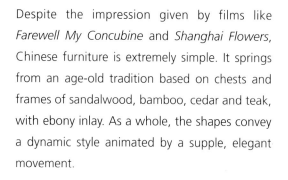

Despite the impression given by films like *Farewell My Concubine* and *Shanghai Flowers*, Chinese furniture is extremely simple. It springs from an age-old tradition based on chests and frames of sandalwood, bamboo, cedar and teak, with ebony inlay. As a whole, the shapes convey a dynamic style animated by a supple, elegant movement.

Small, Song-style ceramic
bowls in "chicken-heart" red (left).
A traditional, stepped storage unit of dark wood
can be used as an attractive room divider (right).
A long console of pale elm features skillfully carved
wings and holds a pewter teapot of ample shape.
The lock on the small central doors evokes
a wedding chest (following pages).

Furniture requiring a framework is naturally highly structured, usually in the form of chests, cupboards, tables and reclining platforms or canopy beds shielded by curtains, all of which are generally trimmed with lacy woodwork. Chairs, meanwhile, with their slightly splayed legs and high, more or less arched backs, are often varnished or lacquered.

A traditional Chinese folding chair displays elegant curves. It comes from a temple where it was reserved for guests. The straight-legged table is decorated with carved scrollwork.

In Japan, the range of furniture is extremely limited. People sit and sleep on the floor, which explains the profusion of mats, usually made of rice straw. The few low tables and cupboards, asymmetrical shelves, book stands and kimono racks are all formally very austere even though materials, colors and patterns are extremely refined.

On the other hand, there are plenty of chests: chests of every size and kind, executed in wood both costly and ordinary, with clear formal simplicity. Sophistication is expressed in the way they are assembled and collected. They can, for example, be combined into steps, partitions or screens.

Quite recently, Japan has opened up to innovation in furniture and forms. Japanese designers, although among the best in the world when it comes to high tech, approach the household realm rather cautiously.

lively finishes

For instance, sculptor Isamu Noguchi's rice-paper lanterns (hung or held by a bamboo stick weighted with a stone), or the "Butterfly" stool by architect Sori Yanagi (simultaneously a stylized butterfly and a three-dimensional ideogram) clearly spring from the Japanese tradition. Although contemporary, these creations seem timeless.

Of Chinese origin,
this picnic basket of carved wood
features a highly worked cover and handle (left).
This low "concubine's chair"dates from the
nineteenth century. Made of stained elm,
its carved back includes both fruit and leaf patterns
and calligraphy (right).
Designers are often most inspired by nature's
simple shapes—a Chinese elm and an elegant fruit bowl
in black lacquer (following pages).

In an entirely different register, designer Shiro Kuramata, although resolutely contemporary, also submits, in his own fashion, to the grand Japanese tradition. His work is, in a way, non-furniture. As Kuramata likes to say, his "furniture should seem to float in space." His very powerful idiom manages to express an aspiration for minimalism and transparence, whether in the form of "Miss Blanche," an armchair of transparent acrylic inset with a scattering of roses, "Side Two," a storage item in the shape of a curling wave, "Solaris," a chest of drawers hung on four sky-bound legs, or "How High the Moon," a deep armchair of wire mesh. They all convey a preoccupation with defining space through light alone, a determination to eliminate any trace of structure from a universe in which the word "decoration" does not exist.

An interior conceived around a Japanese *obi* or silk sash, creates a subtle sense of symmetry. The traditional futon is replaced here by a mattress covered in wine-red cotton, while filtered light creates an atmosphere of serenity for this floor-level setting (right).
Japanese *getas* are made from a wooden sole raised on two wood slats and covered with woven straw (below).

addresses

Below are the addresses of the shops, galleries and designers who kindly contributed to the production of this book.
Most of them have several sales outlets in France and abroad, and will forward their addresses upon request.

AM.PM POUR LA REDOUTE

Tel. 0 803 349 349

Fax. 03 20 69 71 97

See pp. 16 (vase), 22 (top),
125 (cabinet).

——

ASIATIDES

Wholesale trade only

Paris outlet:

P.M. Co Style

5 Passage du Grand Cerf

75002 Paris

Tel. 01 55 80 71 06

Fax. 01 55 80 71 07

pmco.style@wanadoo.fr

See pp. 21 (bottom), 24 (top),
33 (top), 34 (top), 36, 44,
52, 62,63 (door), 67,
68 (tea caddy, furniture),
69, 78, 79, 88, 89, 96,
97 (ribbon), 99, 129, 130,
131, 134.

BAUMANN CRÉATIONS

48 Rue de Grenelle

75007 Paris

Tel. 01 45 49 08 22

Fax. 01 45 49 31 32

Outlets abroad:

TOKYO DESIGN CENTER,

25-19 Higashi-Gotanda, 5 Chome,

Shinagawa-ku, Tokyo 141-0022

CREATION BAUMANN, LTD., 41/42

Berners Street, London W1P 3AA

POLLACK & ASSOCIATES, New York

(Tel. 212 421-8755)

info@creationbaumann.fr

www.creationbaumann.com

See pp. 107 (curtain).

——

BERNARDAUD PORCELAINE

11 Rue Royale

75008 Paris

Tel. 01 47 42 82 66 / 01 47 42 61 51

See pp. 8, 9.

BO

8 Rue St. Merri

75004 Paris

Tel. 01 42 72 84 64

Fax. 01 42 72 85 65

See pp. 20, 64, 65, 125, 143 (teapot).

——

BRÛLERIE DES TERNES

10 Rue Poncelet

75017 Paris

Tel. 01 46 22 52 79

Fax. 01 45 25 15 08

Second outlet, Paris:

28 Rue de l'Annonciation

75016 Paris

See pp. 10, 11, 42 (bottom), 68 (tea).

——

CALLIGRANE

6 Rue du Pont Louis-Philippe

75004 Paris

Tel. 01 48 04 09 00

Fax. 01 40 27 84 08

See pp. 21 (top), 22, 24,
39 (lower left), 72, 117 (paper).
The calligraphic works on pp. 48-49
and 107 are by **Jean-Michel Letellier**
for Calligrane.

———

CARAVANE
6 Rue Pavée
75004 Paris
Tel. 01 44 61 04 20
Fax. 01 44 61 04 22
caravane@caravane.fr
http://www.caravane.fr
See pp. 20, 45, 115.

———

CFOC
170 Bd. Haussmann
75008 Paris
Tel. 01 53 53 40 80
Fax. 01 53 53 40 89
See pp. 3, 7, 17, 27, 28, 29,
33 (bottom), 34 (top), 35, 37,
38, 39 (top right), 40, 41, 46,
52, 56, 58 (top left), 60,
63 (vases), 67, 82, 90, 98, 103,
109, 110, 111, 118 (top),
128, 135, 140.

———

CHRISTIAN TORTU
6 Rue de l'Odéon
75006 Paris
Tel. 01 43 26 02 56
Fax. 01 43 29 71 99
Outlets abroad: CHRISTIAN TORTU,
2-15-12 Akasaka, Minato-ku, Tokyo
TAKASHIMAYA, 693 Fifth Avenue,
New York 10022
See p. 14 (flowers).

CRÉATIONS CARINE TONTINI
POUR EXTRÊM ORIGIN
Tel/Fax: 01 43 49 36 11
Outlets abroad: HARRODS,
Knightsbridge, London SW1
MINT, 70 Wigmore Street, London W1
STREAM, 69 Mercer Street,
New York 10012
List of additional outlets on request.
xtremori@club-internet.fr
See p. 15.

———

DESCHAMPS FLEURS
18 Avenue Niel
75017 Paris
Tel. 01 42 27 98 94
See pp. 78 (Christmas roses),
82 (orchid).

———

DESIGN DONATIEN CARRATIER
POUR TOUS LES HOMMES
Port Saint-Clair 2, Les Quilles
34200 Sète
Tel. 04 67 53 19 53
Fax. 04 67 53 11 43
Outlets abroad: FELLISSIMO, 720 Fifth
Avenue, New York 10009; LIBERTY,
Regent Street, London W1R 6AH
plhfrance@aol.com
See pp. 18 (top, place mat), 30 (top),
31, 54-55, 137.

———

DOM
21 Rue Ste. Croix de la Bretonnerie
75004 Paris
Tel/Fax. 01 42 71 08 00
http://www.dom-ck.com
See p. 116 (paper).

GALERIE ANNE MINET ET LUC
MERENDA
Marché Biron, Stand 62/62 bis
Puces de St. Ouen
75018 Paris
Tel. 01 40 11 33 56 / 01 30 88 54 55
Fax. 01 30 58 54 04
See p. 133.

———

GALERIE FARNÈSE
47 Rue de Berri
75008 Paris
Tel. 01 45 63 22 05
Fax. 01 45 63 68 87
http://www.farnese-gallery.com
See pp. 63 (parquet), 69 (parquet).

———

GALERIE SENTOU
24 Rue du Pont Louis-Philippe
75004 Paris
Tel. 01 42 71 00 01
Fax. 01 42 77 29 65
http://www.sentou.com
Sells objects by **TséTsé Associates,**
Création Sori Yanagi, Collection
Sugaharia among others.
See pp. 8, 9, 116 (bowls), 117, 118
(bottom), 119, 121, 122, 123, 126.

———

KIMONOYA
11 Rue du Pont Louis-Phillipe
75004 Paris
Tel. 01 48 87 30 24
Fax. 01 42 77 30 27
See pp. 5, 18 (bottom), 24 (brush),
42 (top), 47, 57, 58 (bottom), 70,
74-75, 81, 84, 86, 87, 92, 93, 94,
101 (right), 114, 124, 138, 139, 141.

LES COMPTOIRS D'ANNAM
Wholesale trade only
Tel. 01 42 46 72 25
Fax. 01 48 00 00 40
Outlets in France:
BOUTIQUE DES ARTS DECO,
105 Rue de Rivoli, 75001 Paris
(Tel. 01 42 96 21 31) and OLARIA,
114 Rue de la Tour, 75016 Paris
(Tel. 01 45 04 18 87)
See pp. 30 (left), 31, 32.

——

LES JARDINIERS DE VILLEBOIS
8 Rue Villebois Mareuil
75017 Paris
Tel. 01 45 74 71 10
Fax. 01 45 72 67 83
See p. 136.

——

MILLER ET BERTAUX
17 Rue Ferdinand Duval
75004 Paris
Tel. 01 42 78 28 39
Fax. 01 42 78 50 85
See pp. 23, 73, 107 (lanterns).

——

MISS CHINA
3 Rue Française
75001 Paris
Tel. 01 40 41 08 92
Fax. 01 40 41 08 97
*See pp. 18 (fork and spoon), 59,
60, 84 (right), 85, 95, 127.*

——

PARIS STORE
44 Avenue d'Ivry
75013 Paris
Tel. 01 44 06 88 18

Fax. 01 45 83 02 05
See pp. 25, 61.

——

SHU UEMURA
176 Bd. St. Germain
75006 Paris
Tel. 01 45 58 02 55
Outlets abroad:
LIBERTY, Regent Street,
London W1R 6AH
SHU UEMURA SOHO
121 Greene Street, New York, 10012
TAKASHIMAYA
639 Fifth Avenue, New York 10022
BERGDORF GOODMAN
754 Fifth Avenue, New York 10019
See p. 71.

——

SOLS MAJEURS
12 Rue Jacques Coeur
75004 Paris
Tel. 01 42 71 74 28
Fax. 01 42 71 74 29
See pp. 16 (flooring), 19.

——

TANG FRÈRES
48 Avenue d'Ivry
75013 Paris
Tel. 01 45 70 84 20
Fax. 01 45 85 35 55
*See pp. 23, 26, 39 (top left and
lower right), 73, 100.*

——

VIRUS
32 Rue du Bourg Tibourg
75004 Paris
Tel. 01 42 78 85 85
See pp. 53, 101 (left), 104, 106.

ACKNOWLEDGMENTS

Annie Desgrippes and Frédéric Morellec would like to thank Valérie Gautier, Suzanne Tise-Isoré and Nathalie Bailleux
at Flammarion, all of whom provided support for this project, as well as Caroline Chambeau who devised the layout,
and Sandrine Balihaut-Martin and Krysia Roginski.
Heartfelt thanks also go to Pascal Desgrippes from Pleins Feux, Jean-Michel Letellier
(for his valuable help on the history of paper) and Mr. and Mrs. Terzakou, as well as to all
the designers and shop owners whose enthusiasm made this book possible.